The Spirit of
BARBIZON

The Spirit of
BARBIZON
FRANCE AND AMERICA

DANIEL ROSENFELD
ROBERT G. WORKMAN

ORGANIZED BY THE MUSEUM OF ART
RHODE ISLAND SCHOOL OF DESIGN

CIRCULATED UNDER THE AUSPICES OF
THE ART MUSEUM ASSOCIATION OF AMERICA

EXHIBITION TOUR

Monterey Peninsula Museum of Art Association
Monterey, California
June 14 – August 17, 1986

University Gallery
University of Florida
Gainesville, Florida
September 6 – November 1, 1986

Bass Museum of Art
Miami Beach, Florida
December 6, 1986 – January 31, 1987

Owensboro Museum of Fine Art
Owensboro, Kentucky
March 1 – April 26, 1987

Arnot Art Museum
Elmira, New York
May 10 – September 13, 1987

Montgomery Museum of Fine Arts
Montgomery, Alabama
November 8, 1987 – January 3, 1988

Copyright 1986 by The Art Museum Association of America,
270 Sutter Street, San Francisco, California 94108.
All rights reserved.

Edited by James Liljenwall
Graphic design and production:
    Ed Marquand Communication Design
Typesetting: The Type Gallery
Printing: Toppan Printing Co., Japan

Library of Congress Catalogue Card Number 85-073557
ISBN 930295-05-6

Front Cover Illustration:
Winslow Homer
Fishin', 1879
Oil on canvas.
$7^{1}/_{4}$ x $9^{3}/_{16}$ in.
Bequest of Isaac C. Bates

Back Cover Illustration:
William Morris Hunt
La Bouquetière, 1856
Oil on canvas.
$39^{1}/_{2}$ x $32^{1}/_{8}$ in.
Gift of Mrs. S. Foster Damon

Publications of the Museum of Art, Rhode Island School of Design, cited in
the catalogue:

Brown University, Department of Art, *To Look On Nature, 1800-1874,
European and American Landscape*, 1972.

Kermit S. and Kate H. Champa, eds., *Selection V: French Watercolors and
Drawings from the Museum's Collection, ca. 1800-1910*, 1975.

Patricia C.F. Mandel, *Selection VII: American Paintings from the Museum's
Collection, ca. 1800-1930*, 1977.

ACKNOWLEDGMENTS

The collection of the Museum of Art, Rhode Island School of Design is rich in nineteenth-century French and American paintings and works on paper. It is particularly strong in its holdings of works by artists of the French Barbizon School and by Americans who came under their influence. Drawn entirely from this extraordinary collection, *The Spirit of Barbizon: France and America* explores this tremendously fertile period in French and American art. The exhibition presents this material in the broad context of earlier work by such Hudson River School artists as Albert Bierstadt and later Impressionist-influenced work by such American artists as Theodore Robinson, as well as the more Symbolist-influenced work of the French artist Eugene Carrière.

This exhibition has evolved as a close collaboration between the Museum of Art, Rhode Island School of Design, and The Art Museum Association of America. We at the Association are truly delighted to be able to help the Museum of Art share part of its important collection with other museums, university galleries, and community art centers throughout this country. On behalf of the museums on the tour, I would like to thank the Rhode Island School of Design for its generosity in making this collection available for tour.

I would particularly like to thank Franklin Robinson, Director; Robert Workman, Assistant Curator of Painting and Sculpture; and Daniel Rosenfeld, Curator of Painting and Sculpture, for their involvement in and commitment to this exhibition. It has been a great joy working with them on all aspects of the project.

At The Art Museum Association of America, Joanna C. Sikes, Exhibition Coordinator, has developed the exhibition, supervised the production of the catalogue, and arranged all the technical details in preparing the exhibition for travel. Beth Goldberg, Registrar, has arranged and monitored the national tour.

Finally, I would like to thank the National Endowment for the Arts, whose generous support has helped make this publication and this tour possible. NEA funds were also used to conserve a number of works prior to travel, thus assuring the preservation of the works for future generations.

We hope that *The Spirit of Barbizon: France and America* will further the understanding and enjoyment of French and American work of this period and that through such collaborations the resources and collections of American museums and universities may be shared and enjoyed by greater numbers of people.

Harold B. Nelson
Exhibition Program Director
The Art Museum Association of America

FOREWORD

The contribution of the Barbizon artists was a special one: the rediscovery of the everyday, the look and feel of real people and how they lived and worked. These artists perceived a nobility and strength in the peasant and his world, and in the trees and forests around him, but also a mystery, as if they were distanced from their subjects, for all their respect for them. This is a very modern perception, and one can argue that the modern world, artistically speaking, starts here.

Be that as it may, the French Barbizon artists had a pervasive impact on the New World, and especially on the city of Providence, largely through the presence of an energetic dealer, a lively group of local artists, and several perceptive collectors. Because of this historical circumstance, and especially the generosity of one of those collectors, Isaac C. Bates, the Museum of Art, Rhode Island School of Design, has been fortunate enough to acquire a remarkable range of paintings and drawings from the Barbizon School, both French and American. We are indebted to Mr. Bates and the other donors who built this collection, and we are delighted that it is receiving wider exposure through this traveling exhibition.

This exhibition was conceived by Robert Workman, Assistant Curator of Painting and Sculpture, and he and Daniel Rosenfeld, Curator of Painting and Sculpture, have collaborated in making both the exhibition and its catalogue a reality. Many other members of the Museum staff have worked hard to help them in their task, and they deserve our warmest thanks: Linda Catano, Terrell Fisher, Maureen Harper, Deborah Johnson, June Massey, Candace Pezzera, Janet Phillips, Laura Stevens, Robert Thornton, Lora Urbanelli, and Jean Waterman. We also wish to thank the following individuals who lent their assistance and support: Robert C. Vose, Jr., Vose Galleries of Boston; Robert Brown, Archives of American Art, Smithsonian Institution; Barbara Ward Grubb; Harriet S. Magen; and Elizabeth Workman.

Finally, we are truly grateful to The Art Museum Association of America, and especially Harold Nelson, for shouldering the massive administrative burden of applying for the grants, arranging the itinerary, seeing the catalogue through the press, and so much else. Without their generous efforts, this exhibition would not have been possible.

Franklin W. Robinson
Director
Museum of Art, Rhode Island School of Design

THE SPIRIT OF BARBIZON

The village of Barbizon lies at the entrance to the Forest of Fontainebleau, some forty miles south-east of Paris. At the beginning of the nineteenth century, it was an ordinary village of farm laborers, comprising perhaps twenty dwellings. A century later, its name identified the great revolution in French landscape painting that occurred between 1830 and 1880, when the idealization of nature was replaced by the ideal of natural truth.[1] The emergence of Barbizon in the history of nineteenth-century art coincides with the imperative to paint directly in front of nature in the open air (hence the term *plein-air* painting). This imperative drew scores of artists to the wild forest and in the process undermined the classical norms of decorum, finish, and invention. Barbizon painting was part of a broader trend toward naturalism in European painting, poetry, and literature during the second quarter of the nineteenth century and an outgrowth of the romantic dialogue between the artist and nature. The modest desire of the Barbizon artists to paint in the landscape itself was the prelude to Impressionism and modern art.

Because of its proximity to the western fringe of Fontainebleau, the village of Barbizon became the base from which scores of artists departed to paint the varied parts of the great forest. The reminiscences of the painter Stamati Bulgari (active ca. 1789–1840), a pupil of Jacques-Louis David (1748–1825) and a friend of Camille Corot (1796–1875), are among the first describing the presence of artists in and around Barbizon. When he arrived, in 1821, the village had neither an inn nor a path through the edge of the forest (the Bas-Bréau). Bulgari, "who like an intrepid navigator, had pushed ahead as far as this primitive lair," found lodging with one of the peasants, a woodcutter named Père Luche, who for four *sous* a day provided a place near the fire and two peasant meals of soup, bread, and stale cheese.[2] Bulgari's memoirs describe a fellow artist en route to his work in the forest:

> There was something strangely eccentric about his clothes: a big slouch hat shaded his brow and covered his long hair; a smock of grey linen served him both as garment and paint-rag; gaiters of the same material and heavily studded footwear protected his folding stool; in one hand he held a big painting canvas, in the other a spike with which to secure his sunshade while he was working; in a pack on his back he carried a box of paints and an easel. This fantastic get-up attracted the attention of passers-by all along the way and gave rise to gibes as biting as they were good-humored.[3]

This account evokes an image of the new landscape painter of the early nineteenth century: a pioneer living among the peasants, exploring the uncharted wilds of the natural landscape. This was an aspiration far removed from the Neoclassical artist, who was oriented toward the warm south, in particular Rome and its sunlit *Campagna,* which lent itself to the measured description of an idealized style. The French artist who traveled to Rome in the early nineteenth century typically viewed nature from the terrace of the Villa Medici, the home of the French Academy, where the principles of the classical tradition were taught. The artists drawn to the Forest of Fontainebleau left the baggage of tradition behind them.

The early trickle of painters to Fontainebleau was followed by a virtual flood. Artists were attracted to its wild and untouched forest of oak, pine, and birch, to its rocky outcroppings and boulders, and to its surprising vistas—all located a brief day's journey from Paris's crowded streets and the manicured forests at Boulogne and St. Cloud. Georges Michel (1763–1843) may have been one of the first painters to discover the special character of Fontainebleau, and it seems that Corot's first teacher, Achille Etna Michallon (1796–1822), painted there as well. In 1822 an inn was opened at Barbizon by Père Ganne, consisting of "a single storey above the ground floor, a perfectly plain facade with a carriage gate, through which you can see right into a courtyard dotted with puddles and dunghills.''[4] This unassuming country inn—the naturalists' Villa Medici—became the center where artists in the region would congregate and reside, often for the duration of the summer and the fall. Its prominence in nineteenth-century art rivals that of the quarter of the Nouvelle Athènes in the early part of the century, or Montmartre in the fin-de-siècle, and is central to the reorientation of French landscape painting during the middle years of the century. The painters Caruelle d'Aligny (1798–1871) and Corot began to visit Barbizon as early as 1824. Théodore Rousseau (1812–1867) began to paint in Fontainebleau as early as 1826 and, after 1837, rented his own studio in Barbizon, settling there permanently in 1846. Corot exhibited his first Fontainebleau subject in the Salon of 1831 and spent his first full summer in Barbizon in 1835. Narcisse Diaz (1807–1876) met Rousseau there in 1837. Charles Daubigny (1846–1886) began his first major group of works in the forest in 1843. Jean-François Millet (1814–1875), accompanied by Charles Jacque (1813–1894), made his year-round home in Barbizon from 1849 until he died in 1875; and it was there, in 1867, that Rousseau died in Millet's arms. By 1848 Ganne had as many as twenty-eight painters staying at the inn in the course of the year.[5] The Goncourt brothers stayed there on several occasions in the course of writing *Manette Salomon,* a novel of artistic life in mid-century Paris whose heroes, wishing to escape the confined life of the city, sojourn in Ganne's inn.

The Forest of Fontainebleau, however, was not the only part of the French countryside painted by the peripatetic Barbizon landscape painters. Artists combed the length and breadth of France seeking the special qualities peculiar to each place.[6] An important part of the Barbizon phenomenon was not just the appearance of landscape subjects from the Fontainebleau region, but the popularity of French landscape generally, replacing the preference for Italian sites, with their southern light that permitted the rational construction of timeless beauty. Corot, for instance, often painted in the environs of Paris—in particular near his family home in the Ville d'Avray.[7] Rousseau's first famous landscapes were from the Auvergne, and at the same time as his early Fontainebleau work he painted for extensive periods in Landes and Berry. The work of Millet's early maturity is closely identified with his native Cherbourg and Le Havre. Jules Dupré (1811–1889) spent most of his maturity in l'Isle Adam, north of Paris; in his late work he preferred the seascapes of the Channel coast. Daubigny also painted extensively along the Channel, around Lyon, the valley of the Oise, and in Auvers, where he made his home. Barbizon, however, attracted all these painters and many others and came to symbolize the revolution then taking place in French art.

This revolution was a quiet one, in which the weight of a great tradition succumbed to the ethos of self-expression, as reflected in the humble and direct confrontation of nature. At first glance there would seem to be nothing exceptional in the desire of a handful of artists to paint directly in the wilds of nature. Yet, from the vantage point of the early nineteenth century, this inclination foreshadowed the dissolution of a well-established order. Landscape painting, especially in France, had been a minor genre in the late eighteenth and early nineteenth centuries, subservient to history painting, which emphasized the depiction of great deeds from the past and which held that historical, religious, and mythological subjects provided examples of virtuous human behavior that, when rendered in an idealized style, represented a higher order of human affairs. This higher order was conveyed by the rational principles of the classical style as well as by the lofty subject itself. This bias toward classicism, institutionalized by the French Academy and the pedagogy of the École des Beaux-Arts, implied a bias against landscape or, more generally, against what was termed the servile imitation of nature. The erudite artist was expected to improve upon the outward forms of nature; mere imitation was disdained as a rote exercise, lacking the artistic virtue of invention. The heroic style of landscape, influenced by the examples of Nicolas Poussin (1593/4–1665) and Claude

Lorrain (1600–1682), presumed to show nature not as it is but as it ought to be: purged of imperfection, accident, and transient effects, and recreated according to an *a priori* notion of pictorial order.

Although the Academy placed a premium upon invention at the expense of imitation, the direct study of nature, or *plein-air* painting, did have a place within the education of the academic artist of the early nineteenth century. Pierre Henri de Valenciennes (1750–1819), the great Neoclassical landscapist, often sketched in the open air, as Poussin and Claude had before him, and he encouraged his students to do likewise. By sketching in *plein-air,* the artist hoped to capture the transient effects of light and atmosphere, which might later be incorporated into a finished tableau. Valenciennes emphasized that the *plein-air* painting should be executed quickly, its goal being to copy the shifting light of the sun:

> To begin with you should limit yourself to copying as well as you can the principal tones of the natural effect you have chosen. Start your *étude* with the sky, which gives you the background tone; from this advance to the middle distance and by degrees to the foreground, which will thus always be in harmony with the sky, from which the local tone is taken. It is clear that in this way you will not be able to fill in any detail: for all *études* from Nature should be done within two hours at the outside, and if your effect is a sunrise or a sunset, you should not take more than half an hour. [8]

Such studies from nature, however, were points of departure—a means to and not the end of a realized work. The artist's skills of observation and description were an essential part of his knowledge, as was his familiarity with antique art, the classics, and the science of perspective. But Valenciennes still maintained that the superior artists were those who "by closing their eyes ... [see] Nature in her ideal form, clad in the riches of the imagination." [9] The artist was obliged to give nature the appearance of permanence, and it was a consequence of this view that the landscapes submitted to the Salon were inevitably carefully finished studio pictures.

The history of the Barbizon School is the history of painters opening their eyes, observing nature in her actual forms, unencumbered by the burdens of the classical tradition and its view of nature and the imagination. Several factors contributed to this awakening: the decline of history painting and the concurrent rise of Romanticism; a new receptivity to British and Dutch painting; and the social and political consequences of the Industrial Revolution.

History painting, vitally linked to the unfolding Revolution in France but frequently reduced to mere propaganda during the Napoleonic Empire, declined to irrelevance during the Bourbon Restoration. The flowering of landscape painting in the 1820s directly paralleled this decline—a decline abetted by the gradual rise of Romanticism, which placed a higher value on self-expression than on collective ideology, producing a shift from didactic subjects to the private contemplation of nature. The Barbizon painters shared the Romantics' aversion to the artifice of classical landscape and to the formulaic conventions of the picturesque style popular in British painting of the late eighteenth century. In fact, the naturalism of the Barbizon painters may be seen as a product of the particular strain of Romanticism that was influenced by empirical science, as in John Constable's (1776–1837) studies of clouds and Théodore Géricault's (1791–1824) portraits of the insane. [10] Romantic empiricism of this kind was motivated by a desire to penetrate to the soul of nature through contemplation of its outward forms. Similarly, the intimate landscapes of the Barbizon painters were as much concerned with mood as with physical appearance: they were directed less to nature's transitory aspects (the goal of early Impressionism) than to its underlying character, seeking the voice of each landscape site. "Naturalism," Robert Herbert observed, "did not mean a slavish copy of nature, but a felt dialectic between the artist and his subject." [11]

In the early nineteenth century, when it was but a minor genre in French painting, landscape dominated the attention of British painters. One particularly important and conspicuous offshoot of this British landscape tradition was the profusion of topographical landscapes of the French countryside published in prints by British artists. Thomas Girtin's early aquatints of landscapes around Paris (1803) were followed by a flood of travel books illustrating views of Paris and its environs, the Channel coast, and the regions along the Seine and Loire. [12] It was the function of these prints to record specific sites with directness and simplicity, providing an important model for French painters. Equally important must have been the example of John Constable, although the breadth of his influence is difficult to assess. Géricault, who traveled to England in 1820, was familiar with him as was Delacroix four years later. Constable exhibited three landscapes, including his famous *Haywain,* in the Salon of 1824 (among thirty British works exhibited), where he was awarded a Gold Medal and where his works were so popular they were moved to the principal exhibition space—a very high honor for an Englishman in France. [13] The dealer John Arrowsmith showed Constable's paintings in his Paris gallery, and Delacroix's exposure to them there in 1824 inspired him to repaint the background of his *Massacre at Chios,* juxtaposing strokes of pure color to create the vibrancy and luminosity typical of Constable's technique. Constable's great achievement in the simulation of natural effects, the loosening of facture by which this is achieved, and the freshness of his vision— aiming, as he said, to forget that he had ever seen a picture when he sat down to paint before nature—must have served as an important early example of these same concerns brewing among the younger Barbizon painters.

Equally important to the Barbizon painters was the example of seventeenth-century Dutch painting, which became increasingly popular because of its basis in the observation of nature and humanity. The Dutch influence was manifest in three genres that were of lesser importance in the academic hierarchy of pictorial types but which became the mainstay of Barbizon subject matter: landscape, genre (especially important to Millet), and animal painting (especially important to Jacque and to Troyon, who after his trip to Holland in 1847 devoted himself almost entirely to this genre). The Barbizon painters avidly copied and collected Dutch painting, and by the 1830s comparisons between the Barbizon painters and the Dutch Baroque became common to critical reviews of their work. [14] The writings of Théophile Thoré (1807–1869), a close friend and defender of the Barbizon painters, may speak for the entire movement, its principles, and its orientation towards Dutch art. Thoré (writing under the pseudonym W. Bürger) chose Holland for his exile after the collapse of the Second Republic. Between 1858 and 1860 he published his two-volume *Musées de la Hollande,* in which he embraced the humanity of the Dutch school for (in his view) its moral superiority to Italian painting; as he put it, while the latter was enslaved to Christ and Apollo, the former was the art of man:

> The character of Dutch art in general is to be found in life, in living life, man, his customs, his occupations, his joys and whims. . . . This is no longer a mystical art, embracing old superstitions, a mythological art, reviving old symbols; a princely, aristocratic and consequently exceptional art, consecrated exclusively to glorifying the tyrants of this human kind. [15]

Dutch art, rather, was preferred for its adherence to everyday life, replacing the glorification of myth, superstition, and heroes. The political basis for Thoré's turn to Dutch art echoes the underlying political thrust of Barbizon art: to paint what one sees and feels was an egalitarian impulse which stood in conflict with the rarefied orientation of nineteenth-century classical art, steeped in theories comprehensible only to a privileged few.

This egalitarian impulse that came to be identified with Naturalism had its roots in the social conditions of mid-nineteenth-century France, particularly in the urban-industrial revolution. Between 1831 and 1851 the population of Paris and its suburbs doubled, reflecting a vast shift of rural population to this urban center of industrial production and capital. [16] Between 1852 and 1857, to accommodate this dramatic migration to Paris, Baron Haussmann, employed by Napoleon III to rebuild the city of Paris, supervised the erection of 24,000 new buildings and hundreds of miles of roads.

Barbizon art was a response to this radical demographic change. The rural life embodied by the village of Barbizon was the antithesis of the burgeoning industrial city, which threatened a way of life as old as human society. The pursuit of rural life by progressive artists was an effort to find release in nature from the degradation of the urban-industrial environment—its tenements, its factories, and its pollution. Their return to nature was thus made in direct response to changes in the conditions of life, and in this sense their choice of actual, identifiable rural subjects was a modern phenomenon. Unlike the pastoral, bucolic, picturesque, and sublime subjects of the eighteenth century—landscapes of invention and fantasy—these places actually existed, and this reality made them an attainable moral and social alternative.

The passion for nature manifest in the Barbizon phenomenon must therefore also be understood in terms of the corresponding political climate in France during the first half of the nineteenth century. History painting, which espoused timeless values, was undermined by the instability of government in France, where the sequence of Revolution (1789), Republic (1792), Directory (1795), Consulate (1799), Empire (1804), Restoration (1815), Revolution (1830), Republic (1848), and Empire (1853) suggested that nature was more durable than politics. More immediately, the Bourbon Restoration between 1815 and 1830 was a period when official policy toward the arts was narrowly conservative, perhaps in reaction to the inconstancy of previous governments and the values they espoused. It was in this climate of conservative artistic policy that Romanticism germinated, its overtly antagonistic relationship to official policy marking the birth of the avant-garde. By contrast, the more liberal July Monarchy embraced the art of the Romantics, and it was this same Orléanist faction, including the duc d'Orléans himself, who first patronized the younger generation of Barbizon artists.[17] The painters of this emerging generation came to be known as the "men of 1830," and it was during the reign of the July Monarchy that Barbizon art took root and grew.

The triumph of Naturalism occurred with the Revolution of 1848, which had a liberating effect upon progressive artists, who equated their aspirations with the social and political ideals of the Second Republic. Millet, Rousseau, Dupré, and Jacque all fought on the barricades in 1848; Diaz, Daubigny, and Troyon were Republicans as well. The Barbizon painters, whose orientation had formed well in advance of the Revolution of 1848, found in the progressive social climate of the mid-century Republic a confirmation of their longstanding ideals. After 1848 there was a dramatic increase in the depiction of scenes of everyday life. It is noteworthy that Corot, who among the Barbizon painters was the most comfortable in official circles, exhibited a study for the first time in the jury-free Salon of 1849, as well as his first *plein-air* painting of a French site.[18]

"To be of one's own time" became the rallying cry of progressive artists,[19] a phrase that was meant to encourage the rejection of artistic traditions that had been inherited from the past. "We have always been Greeks, Romans, Englishmen ... etc., let's be ourselves for a little while. ... Let us paint only what is, or at least, what we see, what we know, what we have lived. ... A singular school, isn't it? ... whose only principles are independence, sincerity, individualism!"[20] This desire to paint the observable present in a style that claimed to reject traditions inherited from the past was motivated by egalitarian concerns; its moral thrust was suggested some years later by the critic Castagnary, who coined the term "naturalism" to describe the new movement in painting:

> Casting off schools, fleeing systems and preconceived notions, striving to make from immediate things simple, clear art, intelligible even to the most humble, naturalism spurns all that is obscurity, remoteness, enigma—that is to say, everything that addresses itself to the few.[21]

It must be remembered, however, that Barbizon art coalesced far in advance of its embrace by the critics who linked it with progressive social causes. Nevertheless, Barbizon was always viewed as the model of artistic independence and sincerity. Its direct and unpretentious confrontation of nature—and in the case of Millet, its straightforward presentation of peasant life—served as the foundation for the new avant-garde.

Although Barbizon painting can be be viewed as a single phenomenon, the work of its practitioners was diverse, as would be expected of a movement that placed a premium upon sincerity, individuality, and freedom from the past. The work of Georges Michel (cat. nos. 18, 19) is an important early example. At the height of the Neoclassical period in France, Michel (who had been employed to restore Dutch paintings in the Louvre) devoted himself to painting landscapes of the environs of Paris, employing a loosely brushed *plein-air* style that sought to capture the transient effects of weather, atmosphere, and light. For the Barbizon painters, Michel was a model of the artist's ability to find communion with nature in local subjects. "The man who cannot paint for a lifetime within an area of ten miles," he said, "is a clumsy fool who is searching for mandragora and will find nothing but emptiness."[22]

Théodore Rousseau, a guiding spirit of the Barbizon artists, typically worked in a quick, expressionistic style suggestive of his art's Romantic origins (cat. nos. 25–29). Rousseau, who spent most of his time after 1848 in Barbizon, preferred the untamed aspects of nature, which he sought in the solitude of the forest. His increasing devotion to the effects of weather and light (which for him were the "great secret" of nature) made him an important bridge between Constable and Monet.[23]

Corot (cat. nos. 3–6), in spite of the great beauty and originality of his work, was an anomaly among the Barbizon painters. Although he was the first among the group to work consistently in *plein-air,* painting in Fontainebleau as early as 1824, he preserved a devotion to classical subjects and maintained a distinction between sketches from nature and the finished studio picture long after this distinction had been abandoned by his colleagues. Corot was best known to the public through his atmospheric landscapes, strongly influenced by Claude, while his importance in the history of Naturalism is better reflected by his brilliant *plein-air* style, which became increasingly well known in the 1850s.

The work of Diaz (cat. no. 11) shows the strong influence of Rococo art, a consequence of his early career as a porcelain painter. His surfaces were generally painted in a thick impasto covered with glazes, giving his canvases a rich, shimmering effect. Constant Troyon (cat. no. 30) was profoundly influenced by a trip to Holland in 1847, thereafter devoting himself almost entirely to animal subjects, which had a tremendous influence upon the emergence of this genre in later nineteenth-century art. Charles Jacque (cat. nos. 15–18), who devoted much of his time to animal husbandry, likewise specialized in the depiction of animals, in particular sheep.

Millet (cat. nos. 20–24) was the giant of the group and unique among them in his concentration on peasant subjects. After 1849 he made Barbizon his year-round home, depicting the peasants' struggles with the obdurate forces of nature. Of all the Barbizon painters, Millet's works were most closely identified with radical political causes, in large part because of the unflinching realism with which he represented the details of their daily lives. But his subjects, which were a direct response to the Industrial Revolution, were more fatalistic than revolutionary, connoting, as Robert Herbert has observed, the age-old struggle of man for existence.[24]

Daubigny (cat. nos. 7–10) was better known as a printmaker than as a painter, his canvases coming into prominence only after 1850, when he became more closely associated with Corot. Corot influenced Daubigny to work more directly from nature. In 1857 Daubigny constructed a studio-boat, nicknamed *Botin,* which enabled him to concentrate on *plein-air* river scenes. Daubigny was the Barbizon painter most closely allied with the younger generation of Impressionists. His work of the 1860s was increasingly criticized for its directness and lack of finish. In 1861 Gautier accused Daubigny of painting ''an impression,'' offering ''little more than a juxtaposition of spots of color''—thus setting forth the terms on which the battle of Impressionism would be waged. [25]

The legacy of Barbizon was most profoundly reflected in the emergence in the late 1860s of Impressionism, which inherited the mantle of the avant-garde. The high value placed on working in *plein-air*; the desire to paint quickly, in order to capture a direct impression of nature; the disregard for the conventions of finish; the employment of a divided brushstroke in order to simulate the optical effects of light; and the slice of nature that replaced the panoramic approach to composition—all were reflections of innovations employed by the Barbizon painters. The Impressionists took a more detached, ''optical,'' and objective approach to the visible world, and in the process pushed their work decidedly in the direction of abstraction. Ironically, the legacy of Naturalism and the pursuit of a technique that would simulate the transient effects of optical stimuli may have led to the dissolution of the bonds which, since the early Renaissance, had linked painting to the representation of external appearances.

Daniel Rosenfeld
Curator of Painting and Sculpture
Museum of Art, Rhode Island School of Design

NOTES

1. The term "Barbizon School" has been attributed to Georges Lafenestre, who wrote in 1907, with regard to the history of nineteenth-century landscape in France, "The rustic school's most virile effort was concentrated in Barbizon; in fact, nearly all its followers came to know Barbizon, in one way or another. Perhaps in the future, the art critics, historians and art lovers will refer to the landscape painters of the XIXth century as the 'Barbizon School,' just as the portrait painters of the XVIth and XVIIth centuries were referred to as the 'Fontainebleau School.' " See Marie-Thérèse de Forges, *Barbizon et l'École de Barbizon* (Paris, 1971), p. 81.

2. From Alfred Sensier's manuscript notes in the Bibliothèque Municipale de Fontainebleau, quoted in Jean Bouret, *The Barbizon School and 19th Century French Landscape Painting* (Greenwich, Connecticut, 1973), p. 80. See de Forges, p. 82.

3. Stamati Bulgari, *Souvenirs* (1835), quoted in Bouret, p. 82.

4. Pigeory, *Révue des Beaux-Arts,* August 1, 1855, quoted in Bouret, p. 82.

5. Bouret, pp. 87–88. Ganne's willingness to extend credit to artists certainly increased the popularity of his inn. Around 1850, Théodore Rousseau owed Ganne more than 1000 francs, and took over a year to clear the debt.

6. Robert L. Herbert, *Barbizon Revisited* (New York, 1962), p. 16. A quarter century after its publication, Herbert's catalogue remains the most informative work on Barbizon art published in English.

7. He was the only member of the Barbizon group to be attracted to Italy and its classical landscape, having studied there between 1825 and 1828, returning in 1834, and again in 1843.

8. P. H. Valenciennes, *Elémens de la perspective pratique* (Paris, 1800), pp. 338–339, quoted in Albert Boime, *The Academy and French Painting in the Nineteenth Century* (London, 1971), p. 138.

9. Baron Desazars de Montgailhard, *Les artistes toulousains et l'art à Toulouse au XIXe siècle* (Toulouse, 1924), p. 106, quoted in Boime, p. 137.

10. Constable, for example, looked on his painting of landscape as a "science" and his pictures as "experiments." Géricault's portraits of the insane were commissioned by a physician who wished to diagnose the sitters' obsessions.

11. Herbert, *Barbizon Revisited,* pp. 47–48.

12. See John Sell Cotman, *Architectural Antiquities of Normandy* (1820–22); John Gendall and Augustus Welby Pugin, *Vues pittoresques de la Seine* (1821); Augustus Welby Pugin, *Paris and Its Environs* (1831); Augustus Welby Pugin, *Antiquités architecturales de la Normandie* (1854); J. M. W. Turner, *River Scenery of France* (1833–1835); Charles Nordier and Baron Taylor, *Voyages pittoresques dans l'ancienne France* (1824).

13. Herbert, *Barbizon Revisited,* p. 18.

14. Herbert, *Barbizon Revisited,* pp. 18–19.

15. W. Bürger, *Musées de la Hollande,* I (Paris, 1858), pp. 319–26, and II (Paris, 1860), p. X, quoted in Francis Haskell, *Rediscoveries in Art* (Oxford, 1976), p. 147.

16. Robert L. Herbert, "City vs. Country: The Rural Image in French Painting from Millet to Gauguin," *Artforum* (February, 1970), pp. 44–45. The population of Paris in the forty-year period from 1790 to 1831, by comparison, had only risen by about 1½%, or 10,000. Moreover, the national birthrate in this period of rapid urban growth was relatively low: between 1846 and 1856, Herbert observes, the national population increased by only 640,000.

17. Herbert, *Barbizon Revisited,* p. 20.

18. Herbert, *Barbizon Revisited,* p. 39.

19. The term, *"il faut être de son temps,"* has been attributed to Honoré Daumier. See Linda Nochlin, *Realism* (Baltimore, 1971), p. 103ff. The phrase, however, was used as early as 1828 by Emile Deschamps. See Joseph C. Sloane, *French Painting Between the Past and the Present: Artists, Critics and Traditions, From 1848–1870* (Princeton, 1951), p. 54, n. 4.

20. Fernand Desnoyers, "Du réalisme," *L'Artiste* (1856), p. 200, quoted in Sloane, p. 78.

21. Jules Antoine Castagnary, "Salon de 1868," in Linda Nochlin, *Realism and Tradition in Art, 1848–1900* (Englewood Cliffs, N.J., 1966), p. 68.

22. Bouret, p. 29.

23. Herbert, *Barbizon Revisited,* p. 29.

24. Herbert, "City vs. Country," p. 47ff.

25. Herbert, *Barbizon Revisited,* p. 48.

1.
Eugène Carrière
French, 1849-1906

Woman Sewing
Signed at lower right: Eugène Carrière
Oil on canvas. 13″ x 9⅞″

Museum Appropriation. 18.499

Provenance: Dr. R. Meyer-Riefstahl, New York, 1918.

Publication: *Eugène Carrière Retrospective*, Allentown Art Museum, Allentown, Pennsylvania, 1968, cat. no. 30.

Exhibitions: *Eugène Carrière Retrospective*, Allentown Art Museum, Allentown, Pennsylvania, 1968; *Eugène Carrière*, Minneapolis Institute of Arts, Minneapolis, 1970.

2.
Jean-Charles Cazin
French, 1841–1901

Landscape with Windmill
Signed at lower left: J C Cazin
Oil on canvas. 16⅝'' x 14⅝''

Bequest of G. P. Metcalf. 57.232

Provenance: Mrs. Murray S. Danforth and Mrs. S. O. Metcalf;
G. P. Metcalf.

3.
Jean-Baptiste-Camille Corot
French, 1796–1875

Inside a Swiss Chalet, ca. 1850–55
Vente Corot stamp at lower right
Oil on canvas. 10¼″ x 14⅛″

Helen M. Danforth Fund. 54. 175

Provenance: M. C. Rousett; Lord Berners; David Carritt and H. M. Calmann, London.

Publications: Alfred Robaut, *L'Oeuvre de Corot*, Paris, 1905, vol. 2, p. 244; *Museum Notes*, RISD, 1955, p. 14; *Corot, 1796–1875, An Exhibition of His Paintings and Graphic Works*, The Art Institute of Chicago, 1960, cat. no. 70; *Corot, An Exhibition of Paintings, Drawings and Prints*, The Arts Council of Great Britain, 1965, cat. no. 61.

Exhibitions: *Corot, 1796–1875, An Exhibition of His Paintings and Graphic Works*, The Art Institute of Chicago, 1960; *Corot, An Exhibition of Paintings, Drawings and Prints*, Royal Scottish Academy, Edinburgh, and The National Gallery, London, 1965; *Exhibition of Paintings by Jean-Baptiste-Camille Corot*, Wildenstein and Company, New York, 1969.

4.
Jean-Baptiste-Camille Corot
French, 1796–1875

River at Ville d'Avray, ca. 1871–73
Signed at lower right: Corot
Oil on canvas. 12½″ x 18″

Museum Appropriation. 24.089

Provenance: Scott and Fowles, London, 1924.

Publications: Alfred Robaut, *L'Oeuvre de Corot*, Paris, 1905, vol. 3, no. 2105, p. 279; *Bulletin*, RISD, vol. 12, no. 4, 1929, pp. 36–38.

5.
Jean-Baptiste-Camille Corot
French, 1796–1875

Ville d'Avray, 1862
Etching. 3$^{1}/_{16}''$ x 5''
D.3, II/III

Gift of Mr. Henry D. Sharpe. 46.003

6.
Jean-Baptiste-Camille Corot
French, 1796–1875

Souvenir d'Italie
Etching and drypoint. 18¾" x 13¼"

Bequest of Isaac C. Bates. 97.007

7.
Charles-François Daubigny
French, 1817–1878

Landscape, 1871
Signed at lower right: Daubigny 1871
Oil on panel. 26½'' x 15''

Mary B. Jackson Fund. 73.120

Provenance: Private collection, Providence, R.I.

Publication: ''Recent Acquisitions,'' *The Art Journal*, vol. 23, no. 3,
Spring 1974, p. 249.

8.
Charles-François Daubigny
French, 1817–1878

Dray Horses
Signed at lower left: Daubigny
Charcoal. 12¼″ x 18¹³/₁₆″

Gift of the Estate of Mrs. Gustav Radeke. 31.237

9.
Charles-François Daubigny
French, 1817–1878

Le Gue (The Ford), 1865
Etching. 12^{13}/$_{16}$'' x 14^{5}/$_{8}$''
D. 118, II/II

Bequest of Isaac C. Bates. 13.1114

10.
Charles-François Daubigny
French, 1817–1878

Apple Trees near Auvers, 1877
Etching. 7¾″ x 11⅜″
D. 126

Gift of Mrs. Gustav Radeke. 21.024

11.
Pierre Narcisse Diaz de la Peña
French, 1808–1876

Landscape
Signed at lower right: N. Diaz
Oil on panel. 7½'' x 10⅝''

Bequest of Isaac C. Bates. 13.923

Exhibition: *Memorial Exhibition of Works of Art Given by Isaac Comstock Bates*, Museum of Art, Rhode Island School of Design, 1913, no. 80.

12.
Jules Dupré
French, 1811–1889

Cottage in Berry
Oil on panel. 6½'' x 8½''

Gift of Miss Hope Smith. 63.006

13.
Jules Dupré
French, 1811–1889

The Old Windmill
Signed at lower left: J. Dupré
Oil on canvas. 9½″ x 12¾″

Bequest of Austin H. King. 21.447

Publication: *Bulletin*, RISD, vol. 10, no. 2, 1922, pp. 15–16, 19.

14.
Henri Joseph Harpignies
French, 1819–1916

Landscape with a Pond, 1850
Etching. 7⅛″ x 10″

Gift of Mrs. Gustav Radeke. 20.707

15.
Charles-Emile Jacque
French, 1813–1894

Sheep at Rest
Signed at lower right: Ch. Jacque
Oil on panel. 7⅝″ x 11¾″

Bequest of Austin H. King. 21.448

Publication: *Bulletin*, RISD, vol. 10, no. 2, 1922, pp. 15–16.

16.
Charles-Emile Jacque
French, 1813–1894

Sheep and Shepherdess
Signed at lower left: Ch. Jacque
Oil on canvas. 20¼″ x 16¼″

Bequest of Emma G. Harris. 26.401

17.
Charles-Emile Jacque
French, 1813–1894

Girl with Cows in a Stable
Signed at lower right: Ch. Jacque
Black chalk on grey paper heightened with white. 4⅞″ x 8″

Gift of Mrs. Gustav Radeke. 20.480

Publication: *Bulletin*, RISD, vol. 19, no. 4, 1931, p. 69.

18.
Georges Michel
French, 1763–1843

Landscape, after 1827
Oil on canvas. 19⅜″ x 28¼″

Gift of Miss Hope Smith and Brockholst M. Smith in memory
of The Honorable Royal C. Taft. 59.032

Publication: *To Look on Nature*/RISD, 1972.

19.
Georges Michel
French, 1763–1843

Stormy Landscape
Oil on canvas. 14¾'' x 19''

Bequest of Edward F. Ely. 20.070

Publication: *Bulletin*, RISD, vol. 9, no. 3, 1921, pp. 26–27.

20.
Jean-François Millet
French, 1814–1875

Woman Sewing, ca. 1853
Stamped lower right: J. F. M.
Black crayon heightened with white chalk on off-white paper.
4⁹/₁₆″ x 3⁵/₈″

Gift of Mrs. Gustav Radeke. 20.794

Publications: *Bulletin*, RISD, vol. 19, no. 4, 1931, p. 67;
Champa/RISD, 1975, no. 53.

21.
Jean-François Millet
French, 1814–1875

Return from the Market, ca. 1850–1855
Stamped lower left: J.F.M.
Charcoal with stumping on white paper. 6¼″ x 5¾″
Gift of Mrs. Gustav Radeke. 22.097

Provenance: Georges Petitdider; Haro père; Frederick Keppel and Company.

Publications: *Bulletin*, RISD, vol. 19, no. 4, 1931, p. 67; Champa/RISD, 1975, no. 51.

Exhibitions: Statens Museum fur Kunst, Copenhagen, 1914; *Works of Millet*, Phillips Memorial Art Gallery, Washington, D. C., 1956.

22.
Jean-François Millet
French, 1814–1875

Woman Sewing, 1855
Etching. 4³/₁₆″ x 2¹⁵/₁₆″
D. 9, III/III

Gift of Guy Mayer. 49.385

23.
Jean-François Millet
French, 1814–1875

The Shepherdess Knitting, 1862
Etching. 12⁵/₁₆″ x 9⁵/₁₆″
D.18

Museum Appropriation. 21.352

24.
Jean-François Millet
French, 1814–1875

Peasants Going to Work, 1863
Etching. 15$^{7}/_{16}$″ x 12$^{1}/_{8}$″
D.19, VII/VII

Museum Appropriation. 21.359

25.
Pierre-Etienne-Théodore Rousseau
French, 1812–1867

Landscape
Signed at lower right: Th. Rousseau
Oil on paper mounted on panel. 10¼″ x 7½″

Gift of Miss Ruth Ely. 20.071

Provenance: Théodore Rousseau Estate Sale, Paris, 1868.

Publication: *Bulletin*, RISD, vol. 9, no. 3, 1921, p. 27.

26.
Pierre-Etienne-Théodore Rousseau
French, 1812–1867

Landscape, ca. 1850
Stamped at lower left: TH.R
Black chalk on buff paper. 2³/₈″ x 3¹⁵/₁₆″

Museum Works of Art. 56.122.1

Provenance: Komor Gallery, New York, 1956.
Publication: Champa/RISD, 1975, no. 70.

27.
Pierre-Etienne-Théodore Rousseau
French, 1812–1867

Landscape, 1850
Stamped at lower right: TH.R
Black chalk and grey wash on white paper. 3¼'' x 4⅝''

Museum Works of Art. 56.122.2

Provenance: Komor Gallery, New York, 1956.
Publication: Champa/RISD, 1975, no. 71.

28.
Pierre-Etienne-Théodore Rousseau
French, 1812–1867

Riverbank Landscape
Stamped at lower left: TH.R
Quill pen and ink. 4⅝'' x 5⅜''

Gift of the Estate of Mrs. Gustav Radeke. 31.238

Provenance: Théodore Rousseau Estate Sale, Paris, 1868.

29.
Pierre-Etienne-Théodore Rousseau
French, 1812–1867

Chênes de Roches, 1861
Etching. 5¼″ x 8¼″
D.4, II/III

Purchased with a gift from Mrs. Murray S. Danforth. 53.319

Provenance: Marcel Lecomte, Paris, 1953.

30.
Constant Troyon
French, 1810–1865

The Forge, ca. 1860–65
Inscribed at lower left: C. Troyon
Charcoal with stumping and gouache. 19$^{1}/_{16}$'' x 26$^{5}/_{16}$''

The Collector's Account. 72.033

Provenance: B. G. Verte, Paris, 1972.

Publication: Champa/RISD, 1975, no. 81.

THE BARBIZON SPIRIT IN PROVIDENCE

The Isaac Comstock Bates bequest in 1913 to the Museum of Art, Rhode Island School of Design, greatly enriched the holdings of this institution and preserved a collection of nearly nine hundred objects that reflect the habits of collecting in late nineteenth-century Providence. Outstanding among the works in the Bates bequest was the large quantity of French Barbizon paintings and American landscapes inspired by them. Over one-fourth of the works selected here from the Museum of Art belong to the Isaac Bates bequest.

Providence played a central role in the introduction of Barbizon-influenced landscape painting to America. As early as 1852, Seth Morton Vose, a Providence art dealer, was importing works by Corot, then paintings by Troyon and Daubigny, beginning a long and steady flow of Barbizon paintings into Providence and throughout New England. In 1858 William Morris Hunt returned from France, where he had been a disciple of Millet, working in the Forest of Fontainebleau, and set up his studio in Newport. Artists such as Charles H. Davis and George Whitaker studied at the Académie Julian in Paris and with DePaal in Barbizon, making frequent trips to the Forest of Fontainebleau. Both would later teach at the Rhode Island School of Design, founded in 1877. The art and teachings of Millet and Corot provided inspiration for the founding, in 1880, of the Providence Art Club.

American taste in landscape painting before the introduction of French Barbizon paintings is well illustrated by the works exhibited in Providence in 1854 and 1855 under the auspices of the Rhode Island Art Association.[1] Local collectors lent works by European academic artists, copies of old master canvases, and paintings by contemporary American artists. In keeping with then-current tastes, the Association bought Asher B. Durand's *Chocorua Peak* (1855), now in the Museum of Art, Rhode Island School of Design. Durand's representation of a native American scene, painted with careful attention to detail and sharp delineation of forms, exemplifies the Hudson River School style of American landscape painting then prevailing. Between 1820 and 1860, Hudson River School artists painted views of the American wilderness emphasizing the country's vast natural resources. Drawing on the Romantic tradition in European painting, artists such as Thomas Cole and Asher B. Durand saw in the undefiled views of the Berkshires, the Adirondacks, and the White Mountains a visual metaphor both for the sublime and awesome power of nature and for its more lyrical, peaceful, and domesticated aspects. Most American landscapes from this period, such as Durand's *Chocorua Peak,* celebrate the American continent as a benign land of magnificent richness and plenty.

AMERICANS ABROAD: BIERSTADT AND HUNT

By the mid-nineteenth century, some wealthy Americans were looking beyond the obvious chauvinism of collecting only native scenes by American artists to the attractions of European culture. This reorientation encouraged the growth of colonies of American artists in several European cities. One of the earliest art centers was at Düsseldorf in Germany, which attracted a large number of students between 1840 and 1865.[2]

Until this time, most American painters had received their artistic education at home, generally through the study of old master prints and popular landscapes by Claude Lorrain or Salvator Rosa and seventeenth-century Dutch painters. Many artists were trained as engravers, and it was the meticulousness of the engraving process that predisposed many landscape artists to the sharp clarity and focused details popularized by the Hudson River School. The artists who began to travel to Europe for additional training were usually well versed in this native American style, and it was the practiced discipline of the German academies that most clearly reflected a kind of art that would be acceptable back home. American and German artists shared a national pride in the beauty of their native scenery, and the style taught in the German academies, particularly Düsseldorf, was consistent with American preferences in landscape painting in the mid-nineteenth century.

Classes at the Düsseldorf Academy, as described in a letter in *The Crayon* dated June 1858, consisted of four levels: the elementary, drawing after the antique, painting, and composition. All students within the Academy passed from the basic classes to the more advanced at their own pace, beginning with the elementary, where "they acquire the peculiar style of drawing which almost inevitably remains with them through life." This was followed by drawing from casts of "the most famous antique statues, fragments, etc., with a number of casts from life, of hands, arms, legs, and the like." In the painting class, the next level in the sequence of instruction, artists were taught the rudiments of color and technique, working from the nude figure. "Having attained sufficient power over the palette, the student finally reaches the goal—the composition or master class." It was at this stage that invention replaced the servile copy after nature. The rigors of this academic program were taxing. As the article on the Academy observed, "by far the greater number, after struggling half through the Antique, give up the Academy in despair, seeking either more comfortable quarters and fare in an atelier, or going home in disgust." [3]

In 1854 the German-born American painter Albert Bierstadt left his home in New Bedford, Massachusetts, to study in Düsseldorf. Bierstadt's *Westphalian Landscape* (cat. no. 36) was painted in 1856 near the end of the artist's two-year stay at the Academy and illustrates Bierstadt's mastery of the Düsseldorf style—a sharp-focused realism in the details of nature, especially the foliage, an emphasis on draughtsmanship and outline, and a clarity of spatial composition. The Academy emphasized the accurate observation of nature recorded first by the artist with precise preparatory sketches. *Westphalian Landscape* may be the product of a sketching trip made by Bierstadt in Westphalia in 1854 or 1855.

A suggestion of new developments in the way artists looked at and recorded the landscape—developments that were then being actively explored by such French Barbizon artists as Millet, Corot, and Jules Dupré—is contained within the broader vision of *Westphalian Landscape*. Unlike many of the grand and heroic landscapes being painted by artists at Düsseldorf, Bierstadt's work depicts a relatively limited view across a brook to a thick grove of trees and on to the town marked by the church spire in the distance. The technique is consistent with the rigorous training at the Academy, yet the intimate subject, sense of atmosphere in the distance, and selection of details all foreshadow the changes in American landscape painting to come.

Enrollment at the Düsseldorf Academy declined during the early 1860s, in large part owing to the rigors of the curriculum and the decline of the importance of academic methods. Meanwhile, Paris was unrivaled as the international center of Western art. The period 1850 to 1870 has been called the prelude to the great migration of American artists to Paris. [4] It was during these years that American painters were attracted first to Paris and then to the nearby countryside at the Forest of Fontainebleau. Düsseldorf had offered a strong sense of camaraderie among its students and instructors, to the extent that a typical, almost uniform style had emerged. Paris, on the other hand, was the international center of contemporary art, and its diversity of artistic styles and influences, as well as its atmosphere of controversy and innovation, attracted American artists who were no longer challenged by second-generation Hudson River School painting and who found insufficient room for individual expression in Germany.

An American artist who well illustrates the contrast between Düsseldorf and Paris was William Morris Hunt, who played a central role in the introduction of Barbizon art and ideas to the American audience.

Hunt began his European training at the Düsseldorf Academy in 1845, but he found its methods too rigid and too confining. In 1846 he moved to Paris to study at the atelier of Thomas Couture, where he remained to 1852. Independent studios such as Couture's were popular among foreign artists, because of the flexibility they allowed. While Couture insisted his pupils master the rudiments of drawing, he advocated painting directly on the canvas, rather than applying pigment over a drawing. Couture also encouraged his students to preserve a sketch-like quality in the finished painting; Hunt relates that Couture "would not examine a student's easel if the painting appeared to be retouched."[5] Couture's method of building up an image through the successive thin layering of pigment and glazes was quickly absorbed by Hunt. In 1852 Hunt left Paris to work in Barbizon for two years with Jean-François Millet. Hunt's serious interest in Millet had begun when he saw Millet's first version of *The Sower* in the Salon of 1851 and later purchased it; he was introduced to Millet by his Bostonian friend William P. Babcock. The Barbizon experience was a critical time in Hunt's development as an artist, and he later said of Millet:

> When I came to know Millet I took broader views of humanity, of the world, of life. His subjects were real people who had work to do. If he painted a hay-stack it suggested life, animal as well as vegetable, and the life of man.[6]

The seriousness of purpose demonstrated in images of simple peasants engaged in their daily tasks made a lasting impression on Hunt. Millet's approach to his subject—through directness of observation, honesty of expression, and nobility of form—became the artistic goals toward which Hunt was to strive. He quickly abandoned the elaborate glazing methods of Couture, and began to paint his subjects more directly.

Hunt's studies in France and his successes in the Parisian art world encouraged American interest in Paris. Critical to Parisian artistic life was the Salon, where on a regular-basis Americans could see contemporary French and international art. The scope of these exhibitions and the critical response to them were a rich source of aesthetic and intellectual nourishment for students struggling to establish themselves in the art world. American painters naturally participated in the Salons, as did Hunt, who exhibited *La Bouquetière* (cat. no. 44) in the 1855 *Exposition Universelle* along with two other paintings. Hunt started this important canvas in 1851, while studying with Couture, and continued the work after he began his lifelong friendship with Millet. His paintings were singled out in one review as the best in the American section, especially *La Bouquetière* for its "delicious harmonies."[7] After its exhibition in Paris, the painting was brought to America and shown at the National Academy of Design in 1857. The success of this and other canvases painted in France strengthened Hunt's advocacy of the Barbizon aesthetic—of the artist as an interpreter of nature, painting directly from it, selecting intimate views of the landscape that celebrate the dignity of man and his harmony with the earth—and contributed to Hunt's later success as an artist, critic, and lecturer in New England.

Hunt's *La Bouquetière* stands in vivid contrast to Bierstadt's *Westphalian Landscape,* illustrating the differences between the rigorous, controlled draughtsmanship and tight application of paint of the Düsseldorf style and Hunt's combination of the sketchy, multi-layered brushwork and glazing technique endorsed by Couture applied to a monumentalized image of a peasant girl inspired by Millet. Although *La Bouquetière* was begun while Hunt was a student of Couture, and the treatment of subject reflects that tutelage, the painting also reveals Hunt's early sensitivity to Millet's aggrandized peasant images. A small landscape by Hunt entitled *Farm Scene* (cat. no. 45), probably painted during a later trip abroad in 1866 or 1867, further illustrates important differences between Barbizon-inspired landscapes and the Düsseldorf style. This small panel, probably painted directly from nature, echoes Hunt's fascination with charcoal as a means for quick, summary expression; there is nothing mechanical or controlled about this scene of rural life.

THE INTRODUCTION OF BARBIZON PAINTING TO AMERICA

Hunt's greatest contribution to American painting, however, was less in his own Barbizon-inspired canvases than in his role as proselytizer of the Barbizon aesthetic to American artists and collectors. Hunt's return to America in 1854 and his establishment of a studio in Newport in 1856 brought training in Millet's methods of observation and painting to a small group of American art students, including John La Farge and Henry and William James. After settling permanently in Boston in 1862, Hunt used his compelling presence and clever wit to champion the cause of Barbizon painting and its aesthetic concerns there. In his two series of "Talks on Art," Hunt espoused simplicity, directness, harmony, and a love of nature, even in its humblest forms.

At his classes in Newport and Boston, Hunt emphasized freedom of expression, encouraging students to work from memory as well as from the model. Charcoal, a material Hunt had first learned to use while a student of Couture, was the favored medium, and Hunt advocated its use in rapid, sketchlike strokes. Like Couture and the Barbizon artists Millet, Daubigny, and Rousseau, Hunt wanted his students to transfer the expressive handling of charcoal to oil painting. While direct observation of nature was the artist's first inspiration, it was a nature synthesized by the creative process of visual expression; an impression of nature interpreted by the artist and summarily recorded, rather than methodically recreated through meticulous attention to details.

New England was an appropriate location for the introduction of Barbizon ideas, for it was here that Emerson and Thoreau first spread their message of democracy among mankind and in nature. Their fascination with and admiration for nature instilled in the mid-nineteenth-century New England imagination an appreciation for the delicate relationship between man and the natural world, a recurring theme Americans saw in many of these French paintings. The Boston collectors Quincy Adams Shaw and Martin Brimmer, both friends of Hunt, began to buy Barbizon paintings while in France in the 1850s and 1860s, hanging these works in their Boston homes, where they slowly began to expose a wider audience in that city to modern French painting. Brimmer exhibited Millet's *Harvesters Resting* at the Boston Athenaeum in 1854, making it the first Millet painting publicly exhibited in Boston. The first significant exhibition of Barbizon painting, which included works by Hunt and three other Americans, was held at the Athenaeum in 1858. It received little critical attention but was an important first step toward the spread of Barbizon influence in America.

While Hunt preached the Barbizon gospel in Newport and Boston, and while Barbizon paintings began to be exhibited in Boston, the Providence art dealer Seth Morton Vose became the first commercial importer of these paintings in America.[8] Vose acquired his first paintings by Corot in 1852 and exhibited them in his gallery, although none was purchased.[9] In 1854 Vose was importing paintings by Constant Troyon, and by 1857 he owned examples of all the major artists of the Barbizon school.[10] Throughout this period, however, Vose's success in selling these works was limited. He later recalled in an article published in *The Studio* in 1891:

> I liked his [Corot's] pictures from the first time I saw them, and as I had collected a number of them, I thought I would share my pleasure with my friends and townsmen, so I hung them up in my rooms, and asked people to come and see them. Well, they came, but they laughed so at my pictures and made

such fun of my taste, that I took all of the Corots down and put them away, and did not show them again for a long while, except to those who asked particularly to see them. [11]

Vose's purchase of a group of Corot paintings in 1873 for $25,000 must have established him as the largest single purchaser of this artist's work in America to date. [12] When this group was exhibited in 1881, it gave Providence the honor of having the first comprehensive exhibition of works by Corot held in America. [13] Again, none of the works was sold, but Vose's market grew significantly throughout the 1880s, and in the spring of 1887 he sold five Corot canvases for $10,000 each. [14] American taste was at last becoming receptive to the Barbizon style.

Vose did not work alone in importing Barbizon paintings, relying to some extent on the encouragement of Hunt and the services of Thomas Robinson. Robinson was a Providence artist who in 1854 made the first of twenty-nine trips to Europe. [15] His first three trips were devoted to travel and study, working primarily in Paris at the atelier of Auguste Bonheur. Upon his return to this country, Robinson took a studio in Boston and maintained close contacts with the Providence art community. [16] Robinson's abilities as an artist were greatly overshadowed by his contribution to the spread of Barbizon paintings, working as an agent for Seth Vose. Robinson had entrée to the studios of most of the French Barbizon artists, as well as ready access to the studios of Courbet and Delacroix. [17] Clarence Cook later wrote of Robinson:

> He had known all these artists whose names are now household words to the lovers of poetry in painting, and he had known them, not in a dry, perfunctory way, as a dealer knows artists, but as one with the knowledge of art at first hand, and inborn sympathy with artists, can alone know them. [18]

This access to the French masters placed Robinson in a respected and envied position with his fellow artists in Providence, and provided Seth Vose with a choice selection of inventory for later resale in New England and New York. [19]

THE IMPACT OF BARBIZON PAINTING IN PROVIDENCE

Interest in collecting French Barbizon canvases in America was a phenomenon of the last quarter of the nineteenth century. There were no Barbizon paintings at the 1876 Philadelphia Exposition, while at the World's Columbian Exposition in Chicago in 1893 Barbizon painting dominated the French galleries. As industrial fortunes developed after the Civil War, new collectors emerged who found the simplicity and pastoral beauty of Barbizon subjects easily accessible. Disillusionment with the Hudson River School style, with its pre-Civil War images suggestive of manifest destiny, helped encourage the popularity of these isolated, intimate French landscapes. [20] The enthusiasm for Barbizon paintings resulted in a speculative market in their resale, cultivated with great success by dealers such as Vose. As their availability declined with the deaths of key artists, and as competition for their works increased in both France and America, paintings resold at record-breaking prices. A true art craze had developed. [21]

The growth of American interest in Barbizon painting had a great impact on Providence artists, who clearly illustrate the role of this aesthetic in America. The sales catalogues from the 1880s and 1890s of several prominent Providence private collections show that small landscapes by Corot, Daubigny, Dupré, Troyon, and Rousseau dominated local collections. Art collecting was one important, active part of a broader awareness that led to a greater number of exhibitions in Providence, grassroots support for an art school and museum, and responsive local patronage.

It was through local patronage that a small group of artists successfully maintained studios in Providence. Most, like Thomas Robinson, painted in a style that emphasized a personal interpretation of the subject, often derived from Barbizon imagery of nature. Some of these artists were associated with the newly founded Rhode Island School of Design, established in 1877 with the proceeds from the Rhode Island Women's Centennial Commission of the Philadelphia Exposition of 1876. Providence had long been a manufacturing center for textiles, silver, jewelry, and tools, and the artistic training of designers and craftsmen had been a recognized need since the 1854 Rhode Island Art Association exhibition. The Rhode Island School of Design offered broad-based instruction in drawing, painting, modeling, and design, "that they [artisans] may successfully apply the principles of Art to the requirements of trade and manufacture." [22] The need for competent instructors provided a livelihood for many area artists, and fostered a thriving artistic community.

Artists and collectors joined together in 1880 to found the Providence Art Club, established to promote the appreciation, exhibition, and sale of art. The ideas and attitudes of Barbizon artists were very much a part of the thinking of the Providence Art Club's founders, as is evident from an evocative quotation from Jean-François Millet reproduced inside the title page of the Club's first *Members Loan Collection* catalogue:

> We can start from any point and arrive at the sublime, and all is proper to be expressed, provided our aim is high enough. Then what you love with the greatest passion and power becomes a beauty of your own, which imposes itself upon others. Let each bring his own. [23]

Immediately upon its founding, the Art Club contributed significantly to the exhibition of works by contemporary American artists. Often, the paintings were for sale and found their way into local collections. Isaac Bates, the donor of fifteen of the American paintings discussed here, was an important founding member of the Art Club and one of the most active supporters of contemporary art in Providence.

The establishment of the Art Club, the stimulation of interest in contemporary art, and the serious pursuit of painting by both accomplished and amateur artists, were all evidence of a progressive new attitude toward art. Art could be created, appreciated, and interpreted by anyone who could find it within himself to see in art an expression of beauty and truth.

In 1885, a group of Art Club members, at that time mostly artists, created another organization, the A.E. Club ("A.E." standing for Ann Eliza), to prepare and present papers on topics of interest to its members at regular meetings throughout the year. The art of Barbizon was a popular topic, as were discourses on the value of art and art education. Many of these papers were the work of George Whitaker, a Providence artist who had spent time in Paris and made excursions to Barbizon, meeting Millet and Corot. Whitaker's praise of Millet, who had "so keen an insight into human nature that he was enabled to see the very spirits," [24] and his enthusiasm for Corot, who "has taught us to look at nature out of the common-place way" and whose "paintings appeal to the emotions in the same manner that music does through sound," [25] reflect the common tendency to poetic reflection on Barbizon painting.

Exhibitions of recent French art were not an everyday occurrence in late nineteenth-century Providence, although art in area collections was periodically exhibited. Most important of all these exhibitions was the "Loan Exhibition of Paintings in Aid of the First Light Infantry, Providence," held at Infantry Hall, January 18-23, 1886. The 193 works in the show included numerous Barbizon paintings, thanks in large part to the organizing assistance of Seth Vose. The American section was dominated by the works of artists rooted in the French aesthetic, most importantly William Morris Hunt, George Inness, and George Fuller. A Boston newspaper review acclaimed this exhibition as "the most superb loan collection of modern paintings ever seen in New England.... There has been but one exhibition, in fact, in this country which could be mentioned in the same breath and that was the Bartholdi pedestal loan exhibition in New York in 1883. Even that was not so complete in some directions as the exhibition here." [26]

BARBIZON-INSPIRED AMERICAN PAINTINGS

The selection of American paintings in this exhibition presents the best works from the Museum's collection by artists who either traveled to Barbizon or were exposed to the Barbizon aesthetic in the United States. This selection is not a comprehensive survey of American painters who worked in the Barbizon mode but reflects the particular flavor of local collections. [27] Most artists participated in American painting exhibitions at the Providence Art Club or Rhode Island School of Design, and in many cases their work came into the Museum's collection through the Bates bequest.

George Inness was among the first Americans to spend time at Barbizon and incorporate Barbizon elements into his own paintings. Before he saw his first Barbizon paintings at the Salon of 1852, Inness had developed a style of painting that emphasized generalized forms. His pastoral subjects and somber mood resembled the Barbizon style, and the paintings of Rousseau in particular impressed Inness with "their freedom to paint and their casual views of local French landscape." [28] Inness's exposure to this art, rather than providing a source for imitation, released him to explore his own directions.

Autumn (cat. no. 46) is believed to have been painted upon Inness's return from his trip to France in 1854-55. It is immediately striking for its informality of composition, loose brushstroke, and the poetic, suggestive quality of the rural subject—a civilized landscape in place of the untamed wilderness scenes of the earlier Hudson River School. The Barbizon artists' *paysages intimes* introduced a new type of subject to American artists, who had until this time been encouraged to paint the vastness of the land rather than its intimacies. In his mature paintings, illustrated by *Tivoli, Italy*, 1871 (cat. no. 47), and *In the Berkshire Hills* (cat. no. 48), Inness continued to demonstrate his assimilation of the expressive freedom advocated by Barbizon artists in his loose application of paint and diffuse detail.

Other American artists briefly explored Barbizon subjects and technique while developing their own personal approach to art. One outstanding example is the painting by Elihu Vedder entitled *Italian Scene—Pompeo*, 1879 (cat. no. 56), painted in Italy in preparation for an 1880 exhibition of Vedder's works at the Williams and Everett Gallery in Boston. Vedder first visited Paris in 1856, then settled in Florence until the outbreak of the Civil War. He returned to America during the conflict but traveled again to Paris in 1865. Vedder remained there only a short while, haunted by "the vision of Italy ever before my eyes." [29] So he moved to Italy, which remained his home for the rest of his life.

Italian Scene—Pompeo is a rare expression of Vedder's lessons from contemporary French painting applied to a rural Italian subject. The most striking aspect of this work is the monochromatic surfaces of browns and greys and the impact of light upon those surfaces. It is an architectural scene, with only a glimpse at a distant landscape, and as such recalls the early paintings of Corot. Corot often emphasized the stark effects of light on tonal surfaces, and it is Vedder's interest in this that suggests his earlier exposure to Barbizon painting. [30]

Perhaps the finest American landscape painter at the end of the century was Winslow Homer, who had an early but brief exposure to Barbizon painting while in France for ten months in 1866-67. There is no evidence to link Homer directly to a study of French Barbizon artists, but he was very much a part of a larger group of artists who had direct contact with the "men of 1830." [31] During his stay in France, Barbizon painting was prominently exhibited at the Salon. A retrospective of the work of Constant Troyon was held in Paris in 1866, and an important selection of Rousseau's paintings was hung the next year. Homer demonstrated the impact of this material on his painting by expanding his subject matter to include single figures at work in the fields and in a later series of drawings and sketches of children playing in open pastures or quietly enjoying nature. *Fishin'*, 1879 (cat. no. 43), illustrates Homer's mastery of a simple rural subject. Homer's oblique contact with Barbizon art appears to have confirmed his own developing interest in realism and demonstrated to him the expressiveness of paint that first became evident in his works of this period.

The next major artist to find inspiration in French painting was Alexander Wyant. After developing an early interest in the paintings of George Inness, Wyant left America in 1865 to study painting in Karlsruhe, Germany. By March of the next year, Wyant had given up on the restrictive teaching methods of the German academy and traveled to England, where he came under the influence of John Constable, a major inspiration for French Barbizon painters. Wyant's first large landscapes from this period have been called "Hudson River picturesque at its best," [32] although he eventually loosened his touch and reduced his panoramic vision to a more intimate, personal scale. Wyant suffered a stroke in 1873; in order to continue painting, he taught himself to paint with his left hand and reduced his canvas size still further. The Museum's three examples illustrated here— *Landscape, Morning*, 1881 (cat. no. 58), *Landscape*, an undated watercolor (cat. no. 60), and his important *An October Day*, ca. 1888 (cat. no. 59), considered by Wyant's biographer to be one of his greatest canvases, [33]—are typical of the artist's mature style. His unified tone, the diffusion of brushstroke, and the somber, almost foreboding subject of a lush but empty vista across a pasture, earned Wyant a place of honor beside his contemporaries. George Whitaker's comments about Wyant to local artists in 1892 demonstrate his stature at the end of the century: "He became an expert in securing the fugitive effects of nature and as he progressed he left the channel of Talent and rushed into that of Genius—painting ever after from *feeling*." [34]

Not all Americans inspired by the poeticism of French painting chose to depict American subjects. A notable exception was Carleton Wiggins, who first studied with George Inness during the late 1860s and then worked in Paris and Barbizon for an undetermined period beginning in 1881. Wiggins absorbed the imagery of the Forest of Fontainebleau—its great oaks and craggy ledges, its grazing sheep and cattle—and upon his return to the United States later in the decade continued to reproduce these subjects in infinite variation. After he won a gold medal at the Paris Salon in 1894, Wiggins's pastoral landscapes became popular with collectors, which unfortunately seems to have caused his work to become repetitious and formulaic. After 1902, Wiggins spent his summers in Old Lyme, Connecticut, helping to earn that community its brief distinction as the "American Barbizon." [35] The Museum's *Winter Evening in France* was painted in 1882, soon after Wiggins's arrival at Barbizon. Like many of the canvases of the French painter Constant Troyon, whom Wiggins admired, this image is as much a portrait of an animal as a landscape. [36]

Two regional artists who received national acclaim during their lifetime but have only recently been the subject of renewed consideration are Robert Swain Gifford and Dwight Tryon. Gifford began a limited artistic training in his home town of New Bedford, Massachusetts. During his second trip abroad, in 1874, he became interested in contemporary French painting, which he must have seen years before in Boston and New York. Upon Gifford's return from abroad, his earlier romantic style of painting was replaced by cold, somber vistas across the oceanfront dunes of his native New England. *Looking Seaward*, ca. 1882 (cat. no. 40), is typical of Gifford's ocean landscapes. While the strong horizontal format and large proportion of sky to land and sea recall traditional Dutch marine compositions, the free handling of the paint, the limited palette, and the sobriety of mood reveal his interest in the paintings of Rousseau and Dupré.

Gifford's greatest contribution to American art was perhaps as an etcher. Gifford began etching about 1865, although his initial interest in the process waned until he once again took up the craft in 1877. He was a founder of the New York Etching Club in March 1877. [37] *Landscape*, 1878 (cat. no. 41), was executed the following year and fully demonstrates the artist's expressive use of the etching process. In 1883, the influential art critic Marianna G. van Rensselaer wrote of Gifford, "there is not one among them [our best etchers] who shows a truer feeling for the requirements of this peculiar art than Mr. Gifford...who etches more truly in the etcher's spirit; who knows so exactly what to omit and what to insist upon, and thus produces such complete effects by such simple and synthetic means."[38] James D. Smillie, a contemporary of Gifford's, a fellow organizer of the New York Etching Club, and its later president, applied the etcher's technique to a variety of subjects, including popular pastoral scenes such as *A Fallow Field*, 1883 (cat. no. 52), and *Landscape and Sheep* (cat. no. 53), a copy after a painting by Charles Jacque and directly inspired by the current popularity of Barbizon painting.

Dwight Tryon was a member of a small group of American artists who had direct contact with the French painter Charles François Daubigny in 1876. Daubigny was fascinated with the effects of light on flowing water and spent a great deal of time aboard his boat *Botin*, which served as his studio. Tryon admired Daubigny's free and vigorous handling of paint and later developed a similar passion for depicting water, often making sketches of the shoreline from a boat. *Daybreak* (cat. no. 55) was composed while aboard a fishing boat moored in New Bedford harbor, then painted from memory over the next few days in Tryon's studio in South Dartmouth, Massachusetts.[39] Like much of French Barbizon painting, it is a composition dominated by its strong horizontality—a wide foreground of water, the narrow band of shore, and the expansive sky. These three bands, painted in a broad impasto that recalls Tryon's earlier study of French painting, suggest the varying effects of light on water, land, and sky.

During the 1880s and 1890s, many American artists applied the experimental looseness of brush, tonal coloring, and poetic sentiment of Barbizon art to their regional landscapes. Most achieved only minor recognition, largely because of the imitative and repetitive quality of these paintings. The landscapes of Charles H. Miller, George Smillie, J.N. Barnsley, Eugene Smyth, and Charles H. Davis typify the broad appeal of Barbizon art. Their paintings in this exhibition demonstrate the variety of personal interpretations of the Barbizon aesthetic by Americans, while at the same time revealing a similarity in their choice of subject, range of palette, and moody, dramatic atmosphere.

Perhaps the most noteworthy figure among the Providence artists was Edward Mitchell Bannister, the first Black artist to receive national recognition, with a bronze medal at the 1876 Centennial Exposition in Philadelphia. Bannister admired Barbizon painting, spoke highly of the poetic sentiment of Millet in particular, and was inspired by Barbizon style, which influenced his own deeply religious view of nature. Bannister believed his depictions of the bucolic landscape provided evidence of God's presence in the world.[40] He generally focused on the depiction of weather as a metaphor for the relationship between man and nature: just as the weather is unpredictably in flux, so too is the delicate balance between man and his environment, as well as the relationship of the soul to God.

This sense of changing mood is illustrated by his paintings *At the Oakside Beach* (cat. no. 31) and *Landscape*, 1882 (cat. no. 32). Bannister often painted the marshlands and pastures along the shores of Narragansett Bay, balancing his treatment of the wild and overgrown fields with his depictions of the effects of weather on land, sea, and sky. Light, as it filters through the clouds, reflects across the marshes and illuminates the foreground, enlivening Bannister's quiet landscapes with activity and the sense of change.

Interest in contemporary developments in French painting, particularly in the work of Edouard Manet and Claude Monet, began to be subtly visible in the brightening palette of many contemporary Americans and was often first applied to more traditional Barbizon-inspired subjects, such as scenes of rural life. The Providence artist Sydney R. Burleigh (cat. no. 37) gained a local reputation for his watercolor views of the Rhode Island landscape, as well as his involvement in the Arts and Crafts Movement. In the late 1870s Burleigh traveled to Europe and settled in Paris. For the next two years he studied painting with Jean-Paul Laurens, worked for a period in Italy, and traveled throughout Europe. Upon his return from Europe in 1880 he set up a studio in Providence, and became a leader among Providence artists for the next fifty years. His paintings, which reflect his French training and his endorsement of Barbizon and Impressionist painting, often are intimate views of farmers in their fields and orchards, painted with short brushstrokes in bright colors.

Even as the Barbizon aesthetic took hold in America in the 1880s, innovative American painters were keeping abreast of recent developments in French art, particularly Impressionism. Artists began to use Impressionist technique, as in the work of the English-born Providence artist John Noble Barlow. Barlow's ambitious canvas, *La Moisson, Normandie* (cat. no. 33), was painted while the artist was working in Paris in 1889. This work, and *A Hayfield, Hampshire*, ca. 1902 (cat. no. 34), are painted in a bright palette of soft blues, greens, and yellows that emphasizes the effects of sunlight on the fields and summer sky and moves away from the more traditional muted Barbizon tonality of dark greens and browns. While Barlow was progressive in his use of color, he was more conservative in the application of paint. His brushstrokes merge into one another in a manner more reminiscent of the Barbizon painter Daubigny than of Impressionist artists. Also, the rural subjects of farmers haying or a girl enjoying a rest in the fields derives more from Millet than from the Impressionists.

The eventual shift in interest by American artists from the dark, muted palette and agrarian subjects of Barbizon to Impressionist color experiments, broken touch, and urban or suburban subjects is exemplified in the paintings of Theodore Robinson. When Robinson first traveled to France in 1876, he followed the course of other Americans and studied with the French artist Carolus-Duran and later at the École des Beaux-Arts, where he was trained in academic realism. Unlike the Americans who followed the path to Barbizon, Robinson came under the influence of Claude Monet, spending time at Giverny with the French master beginning in 1888. *Afternoon Shadows* (cat. no. 50) was painted at Giverny in 1891 and follows Monet's example, both in the broken touches of high-key color and in the choice of subject, inspired by Monet's haystack series of the same year. Like Monet, Robinson focused on the changing effects of light on a modest scene, empty of people. It was for paintings such as this that Robinson was credited with what John I.H. Baur called "the wedding of French Impressionism to American art." [41]

Robinson's paintings signaled the new interest in contemporary developments in France that quickly overshadowed the Barbizon painters. In the previous four decades, however, not only had the French Barbizon artists had a great impact on countless American artists and collectors, but the city of Providence had matured into an active art center in New England. Its patronage of contemporary art, which had begun primarily with the French Barbizon landscapes imported by Seth Vose, gradually expanded to include contemporary American paintings exhibited at the Art Club and Rhode Island School of Design. Important loan exhibitions were held, and a movement to establish a museum for the permanent exhibition of art eventually led to the founding of the School of Design and its Museum. Many of the collections amassed during this period became the core of this institution. Barbizon painting—both French and American—thus played a critical role in the development of the Providence art community during the last half of the nineteenth century.

Robert G. Workman
Assistant Curator of Painting and Sculpture
Museum of Art, Rhode Island School of Design

NOTES

1. This was chartered by the Rhode Island General Assembly in 1854 to establish ''a permanent Art Museum and Gallery of the Arts of Design . . . and to use all other appropriate means for cultivating and promoting the Ornamental and Useful Arts.'' See Charter of the Rhode Island Art Association as quoted in Carla Mathes Woodward, ''Acquisition, Preservation, and Education: A History of the Museum,''*A Handbook of the Museum of Art, Rhode Island School of Design* (Providence, 1985), p. 11.

2. For more information on Americans in Düsseldorf, see Anneliese Harding and Brucia Witthoft, *American Artists in Düsseldorf: 1840-1865* (Framingham, Massachusetts, 1982).

3. ''L,'' ''The Düsseldorf Academy,'' *The Crayon*, vol. 5, no. 8 (August 1858), pp. 228-230.

4. See Lois Fink, ''American Artists in France,'' *American Art Journal* 5 (November 1973), pp. 32-49.

5. Albert Boime, *The Academy and French Painting in Nineteenth Century France* (London, 1971), p. 73.

6. Helen M. Knowlton, *Art-Life of William Morris Hunt* (Boston, 1899), p. 12.

7. Anonymous review, as cited in Patricia C.F. Mandel, *Selection VII: American Paintings from the Museum's Collection, ca. 1800-1930* (Providence, 1977), p. 155.

8. There are numerous early references to Vose's involvement with Barbizon paintings; the first modern reference is in G.W. Constable, *Art Collecting in the United States of America: An Outline of a History* (London and New York, 1964), p. 72. More recently, a good discussion of Vose was included in Peter Bermingham, *American Art in the Barbizon Mood* (Washington, D.C., 1975), pp. 44-45.

9. René Brimo, *L'Evolution du Goût aux États-Unis: d'après l'histoire des collections* (Paris, 1938), p. 57.

10. Joan Weakley, *The Art Dealer and His Effect on the Determination of Popular Taste in Paintings: An Analysis of Vose Galleries of Boston, Inc. and Its Influence on American Tastes, 1850-1880* (unpublished manuscript in the files of the Vose Galleries of Boston, Inc., 1978), pp. 3-4.

11. Clarence Cook, ''Art in Providence,'' *The Studio*, vol. 6, no. 21 (April 25, 1891), p. 201.

12. I am grateful to Barbara Ward Grubb for sharing her unpublished manuscript *A Study in Taste: The American Response to Corot, 1852 to 1900* (1979). Also see Seth Morton Vose, obituary, *The Evening Bulletin*, Providence (April 4, 1910), p. 3.

13. Grubb, p. 67. Vose is recorded as having owned in that year at least 165 works by Corot and 69 paintings by Charles-François Daubigny. See Seth Morton Vose, obituary, *American Art News* (May 1910), p. 8.

14. *Evening Bulletin* obituary, p. 3.

15. Edward S. Allen, in *Thomas Robinson, A Memoir* (Providence, 1888), the primary biographical source on Robinson, says that Robinson traveled to Europe 18 times. A copy of this book in the Vose Galleries of Boston, Inc., archives, inscribed in Seth Vose's hand, notes, ''He went to Europe twenty-nine (29) times.''

16. Bermingham, p. 166.

17. Bermingham, p. 40.

18. Cook, p. 202.

19. The association between Vose and Robinson came to an unhappy end in 1888. Robinson was known to suffer from ''manifestations of true mental disease: and was also fond of liquor and gambling.'' During his last trip to Europe, he squandered away $100,000 Vose had sent him for the purchase of art. In an attempt to conceal the loss, Robinson shipped a quantity of fakes to Vose, who confronted Robinson with the deception on his return to Providence. Robinson died shortly thereafter, possibly a suicide. See Robert C. Vose, Jr., ''Boston's Vose Galleries: A Family Affair,'' *Archives of American Art Journal*, vol. 21, no. 1 (1981), p. 16.

20. Aline B. Saarinen, *The Proud Possessors: The Lives, Times and Tastes of Some Adventurous American Art Collectors* (New York, 1958), pp. 14-15.

21. Articles on the front pages of New York papers during the 1890s and early 1900s listed the latest record prices paid for Barbizon paintings sold at auction the evening before. An excellent collection of these clippings can be found in the scrapbook of the Vose Galleries of Boston, Inc., Archives of American Art, Smithsonian Institution, microfilm roll number B 1.

22. ''By-Laws of the Rhode Island School of Design,'' as quoted in Woodward, p. 11.

23. *Members Loan Collection*, Providence Art Club, February 11, 1881.

24. George W. Whitaker, ''J.F. Millet, the Peasant Painter,'' April 21, 1887, address number 40 given before the A.E. Club, Manuscript Library, The Rhode Island Historical Society.

25. George W. Whitaker, ''The Life and Work of Corot,'' June 3, 1897, address number 315 given before the A.E. Club, Manuscript Library, The Rhode Island Historical Society.

26. ''Art in Providence,'' *Boston Daily Advertiser* (January 25, 1886), p. 3.

27. For a thorough overview of this subject, see Bermingham.

28. Wanda M. Corn, *The Color of Mood: American Tonalism 1880-1910* (San Francisco, 1972), p. 6.

29. As quoted in Gloria-Gilda Deak, *Kennedy Galleries' Profiles of American Artists* (New York, 1981), p. 241.

30. Mandel, p. 170.

31. Bermingham, p. 52-53.

32. Bermingham, p. 56.

33. Eliot Clark, *Sixty Paintings by Alexander H. Wyant* (New York, 1920), p. 67.

34. George W. Whitaker, ''Alexander Hamilton Wyant,'' December 1, 1892, address number 181 given before the A.E. Club, Manuscript Library, The Rhode Island Historical Society.

35. Jeffery W. Anderson, *Old Lyme: The American Barbizon* (Old Lyme, Connecticut, 1982), p. 6.

36. Mandel, p. 174.

37. For more information see Maureen C. O'Brian and Patricia C.F. Mandel, *The American Painter-Etcher Movement* (Southampton, New York, 1984), p. 28.

38. Marianna G. van Rensselaer, "American Etchers," *The Century Magazine*, vol. 25, no. 4 (February 1883), p. 494.

39. Mandel, pp. 68-69.

40. George W. Whitaker, "Reminiscences of Providence Artists," *Providence Magazine, The Board of Trade Journal*, vol. 26, no. 2 (February 1914), p. 139.

41. Deak, p. 207.

31.
Edward Mitchell Bannister
American, 1828–1901

At the Oakside Beach, ca. 1877
Signed at lower left: E. M. Bannister
Oil on canvas. 8″ x 12″

Bequest of Isaac C. Bates. 13.829

Publication: Mandel/RISD, 1977, pp. 57–59.

Exhibitions: *Loan Exhibition in Aid of First Light Infantry*, Providence, 1880, cat. no. 119; *Memorial Exhibition of Works of Art Given by Isaac Comstock Bates*, Museum of Art, Rhode Island School of Design, 1913, cat. no. 3; *Bannister and Duncanson, 19th Century Afro-American Artists*, Special Exhibition of the Museum of the National Center of Afro-American Artists, Museum of Fine Arts, Boston, 1972; *Four from Providence: Bannister, Prophet, Alston, Jennings*, Rhode Island College Gallery, 1978.

32.
Edward Mitchell Bannister
American, 1828–1901

Landscape, 1882
Signed at lower right: E. M. Bannister 82
Oil on canvas. 16^1/$_{16}$″ x 22^1/$_8$″
Bequest of Isaac C. Bates. 13.901

Publications: *Edward Mitchell Bannister, 1828–1901, Providence Artist,* Frederick Douglass Institute, Washington, D.C., 1966, cat. no. 16; *Afro-American Artists, 1800–1969,* Civic Art Center Museum, Philadelphia, 1969, cat. no. 21; *Black American Artists in Historical Perspective,* Black Dimensions in Art Inc., Schenectady and Albany, New York, 1976, cat. no. 3.

Exhibitions: *Edward Mitchell Bannister, 1828–1901, Providence Artist,* Frederick Douglass Institute, Washington, D. C., 1966; *Dimensions of Black Art,* La Jolla Museum of Art, La Jolla, California, 1970; *Bannister and Duncanson, 19th Century Afro-American Artists,* Special Exhibition of the Museum of the National Center of Afro-American Artists, Museum of Fine Arts, Boston, 1972; *Black American Artists in Historical Perspective,* Schenectady Museum, Schenectady, New York; Albany Institute of History and Art, Albany, New York, 1976.

33.
John Noble Barlow
American, 1861–1917

The Harvest, Normandy, 1889
Signed at lower right: J. N. Barlow, Paris 1889
Oil on canvas. 39¼'' x 79''

Gift of Hugh MacColl in memory of his father James R.
MacColl. 39.092

34.
John Noble Barlow
American, 1861–1917

Hayfield, Hampshire, ca. 1902
Signed at lower right: J. Noble Barlow
Oil on canvas. 24″ x 32″

Bequest of Isaac C. Bates. 13.903

Publication: Mandel/RISD, 1977, p. 86.

Exhibitions: *Exhibition of Eminent American and Foreign Artists,*
Providence Art Club, 1902; *Catalogue of Oil Paintings by John Noble
Barlow R.B.A. of Cornwall, England,* Museum of Art, Rhode Island
School of Design, 1903.

35.
James M. Barnsley
American, b. Canada, 19th century

Landscape, 1888
Signed at lower right: J. N. Barnsley 1888
Oil on canvas. 12¼″ x 20″

Gift of Jesse H. Metcalf. 52.105

36.
Albert Bierstadt
American, 1830–1902

Westphalian Landscape, 1856
Signed at lower left: A. Bierstadt 18(5)6
Oil on canvas. 24″ x 30″

Gift of Ellen D. Sharpe. 40.188

Publications: *To Look on Nature/*RISD, 1972; Gordon Hendricks, *Albert Bierstadt, Painter of the American West,* New York, 1974; Mandel/RISD, 1977, pp. 34–36.

Exhibition: *To Look on Nature, 1800–1874, European and American Landscape,* Museum of Art, Rhode Island School of Design, 1972.

37.
Sydney Richmond Burleigh
American, 1853–1931

Little Compton, Rhode Island, ca. 1900–10
Oil on canvas. 10¾'' x 15''

Bequest of Isaac C. Bates. 13.917

38.
Charles H. Davis
American, 1856–1933

Full-Tide of Autumn, ca. 1911–12
Signed at lower left: C. H. Davis
Oil on canvas. 25″ x 30″
Jesse H. Metcalf Fund. 27.200

Provenance: Robert C. Vose, Boston, 1920.

Publications: *Catalogue of the Annual Exhibition of Recent American Paintings,* Museum of Art, Rhode Island School of Design, 1927; Mandel/RISD, 1977, pp. 94–95.

Exhibitions: *Paintings by Charles H. Davis, Paul Dougherty, Ben Foster, William Sartain, Gardner Symons, F. Ballard Williams,* Macbeth Gallery, New York, 1912, cat. no. 3; *Annual Exhibition of Recent American Paintings,* Museum of Art, Rhode Island School of Design, 1927.

39.
Charles H. Davis
American, 1856–1933

At Twilight
Signed at lower left: C. H. Davis
Oil on canvas. 17″ x 20⅞″

Gift of Mrs. Gustav Radeke. 20.284

Provenance: Macbeth Gallery, New York.

40.
Robert Swain Gifford
American, 1840–1905

Looking Seaward, ca. 1882
Signed at lower right: R. Swain Gifford
Oil on canvas. 10⅜″ x 22⅛″

Bequest of Isaac C. Bates. 13.794

Provenance: Bought from the artist by Isaac C. Bates, 1882.

Publication: Mandel/RISD, 1977, pp. 63–65.

Exhibitions: *Third Annual Exhibition*, Providence Art Club, 1882, no. 92; *Memorial Exhibition of Works of Art Given by Isaac Comstock Bates*, Museum of Art, Rhode Island School of Design, 1913, cat. no. 25.

41.
Robert Swain Gifford
American, 1840–1905

Landscape, 1878
Etching. 5″ x 9″

Bequest of Isaac C. Bates. 13.1115

42.
Eugene Higgins
American, 1874–1958

The Wounded Tree
Signed at lower right in margin: Eugene Higgins Imp.
Etching. 5$^1/_2''$ x 6$^5/_{16}''$

Gift of Mrs. Gustav Radeke. 24.409

43.
(Illustrated on Front Cover)
Winslow Homer
American, 1836–1910

Fishin', 1879
Signed at lower left: Homer 1879
Oil on canvas. 7$^1/_4''$ x 9$^3/_{16}''$

Bequest of Isaac C. Bates. 13.935

Publications: *Bulletin*, RISD, vol. 5, no. 3, 1917, pp. 18–19;
Mandel/RISD, 1977, pp. 172–173.

Exhibitions: *Memorial Exhibition of Works of Art Given by Isaac
Comstock Bates*, Museum of Art, Rhode Island School of Design,
1913, cat. no. 33; *Winslow Homer, Albert Ryder, Thomas Eakins*,
Museum of Modern Art, New York, 1930, cat. no. 21; *Centenary
Exhibition of the Works of Winslow Homer*, Carnegie Institute,
Pittsburgh, 1937, cat. no. 19; *Winslow Homer in New York State*,
Storm King Art Center, Mountainville, New York, 1963, cat.
no. 5.

44.
(Illustrated on Back Cover)
William Morris Hunt
American, 1824–1879

La Bouquetière, 1856
Signed at lower right: Wm. M. Hunt, 1856
Oil on canvas. 39½″ x 32⅛″

Gift of Mrs. S. Foster Damon. 72.177

Provenance: The artist, 1857; James Davis, Boston, 1879; Henry
Winsor, Boston, 1894; Mrs. Edmund M. Wheelwright, Boston,
1924.

Publications: Frederic P. Vinton, ''William Morris Hunt.—The
Memorial Exhibition.—The Paintings at Albany,'' *The American
Art Review*, 1, 1880, pp. 93–103; Mandel/RISD, 1977, pp.
155–158; *Museum Notes*, RISD, 1980, p. 21.

Exhibitions: *Exposition Universelle*, Paris, 1855; National Academy
of Design, New York, 1857, cat. no. 88; *First Annual Exhibition*,
Washington Art Association, Washington, D.C., 1857, cat. no.
118; *Chronological Exhibition of American Art*, Brooklyn Art
Association, Brooklyn, 1872, cat. no. 73; *Memorial Exhibition of the
Works of William Morris Hunt*, Museum of Fine Arts, Boston, 1924,
cat. no. 19.

45.
William Morris Hunt
American, 1824–1879

Farm Scene, ca. 1866–67
Oil on canvas. 6″ x 8¼″

Bequest of Isaac C. Bates. 13.789

46.
George Inness
American, 1825–1894

Autumn, 1856–60
Signed at lower right: G. Inness
Oil on canvas. 14½″ x 12¼″

Bequest of Isaac C. Bates. 13.805

Publications: *Bulletin*, RISD, vol. 1, no. 2, 1913, p. 11; Leroy Ireland, *The Works of George Inness, An Illustrated Catalogue Raisonné*, University of Texas Press, 1965, cat. no. 138; Nicolai Cikovsky, Jr., *George Inness*, New York, 1971; *To Look on Nature/* RISD, 1972.

Exhibitions: *Memorial Exhibition of Works of Art Given by Isaac Comstock Bates*, Museum of Art, Rhode Island School of Design, 1913, cat. no. 35; *To Look on Nature*/RISD, 1972.

47.
George Inness
American, 1825–1894

Tivoli, Italy, 1871
Signed at lower left: G Inness 1871
Oil on canvas. 25⅛″ x 21″

Gift of Mrs. Jesse H. Metcalf. 95.003

Provenance: Estate of the artist, 1895.

Publications: Leroy Ireland, *The Works of George Inness*, University of Texas Press, 1965, cat. no. 534; Nicolai Cikovsky, Jr., *George Inness*, New York, 1971, cat. no. 44; Mandel/RISD, 1977, p. 46.

Exhibitions: *Inness Memorial Exhibition*, Fine Arts Building, New York, 1894, cat. no. 151; Inness Executor's Sale, Fifth Avenue Art Galleries, New York, 1895, cat. no. 53; *Paintings and Engravings on View at the Rhode Island School of Design at the Opening of the New Galleries*, Museum of Art, Rhode Island School of Design, 1897, cat. no. 45; *George Inness, An American Landscape Painter, 1825–1894*, The George Walter Vincent Smith Art Museum, Springfield, Massachusetts, 1946, cat. no. 22.

48.
George Inness
American, 1825–1894

In the Berkshire Hills, ca. 1875–78
Signed at lower right: Geo. Inness
Oil on canvas. 29¾″ x 44½″

Jesse H. Metcalf Fund. 09.085

Provenance: J. A. S. Monks, 1899; Vose Gallery, Boston, 1899.

Publications: Leroy Ireland, *The Works of George Inness*, University of Texas Press, 1965, cat. no. 849; Mandel/RISD, 1972, pp. 56–58.

Exhibitions: *Second Exhibition*, Kurtz Gallery, New York, 1879; *Panama-Pacific International Exposition*, San Francisco, 1915.

49.
Charles H. Miller
American, 1842–1922

Autumn Landscape, Long Island, ca. 1879
Signed at lower right: C. H. Miller
Oil on panel. 5⅞″ x 11⅞″

Bequest of Isaac C. Bates. 13.943

Publication: Mandel/RISD, 1977, pp. 62–63.

Exhibitions: *Second Exhibition*, Kurtz Gallery, New York, 1879,
cat. no. 140; *Members' Loan Collection*, Providence Art Club, 1881,
cat. no. 16.

50.
Theodore Robinson
American, 1852–1896

Afternoon Shadows, 1891
Signed at lower left: Th. Robinson 1891
Oil on canvas. 18¼″ x 21⅞″

Gift of Mrs. Gustav Radeke. 20.206

Provenance: Silas S. Dustin; William T. Evans, 1911.

Publications: John I. H. Baur, *Theodore Robinson 1852–1896*, Brooklyn Museum, Brooklyn, 1946, cat. no. 2; *Theodore Robinson 1852–1896*, Baltimore Museum of Art, Baltimore, 1973, cat. no. 35; Mandel/RISD, 1977, pp. 78–79; *American Impressionism*, Henry Art Gallery, University of Washington, Seattle, traveling exhibition, 1980; Laura L. Meiner, *An International Episode: Millet, Monet, and Their American Counterparts*, Memphis, 1982, cat. no. 48.

Exhibitions: Newport Art Association, 1948; *Theodore Robinson, American Impressionist (1852–1896)*, Kennedy Galleries, New York, 1966; *Theodore Robinson 1852–1896*, Baltimore Museum of Art, Baltimore, traveling exhibition, 1973, cat. no. 35; *American Impressionism*, Henry Art Gallery, University of Washington, Seattle, 1980; *An International Episode: Millet, Monet and Their American Counterparts*, Dixon Gallery and Gardens, Memphis, traveling exhibition, 1982, cat. no. 48.

51.
George H. Smillie
American, 1840–1921

Hillside, 1883
Signed at lower left: Geo. H. Smillie—1883
Oil on canvas. 9″ x 16″

Bequest of Isaac C. Bates. 13.949

Publications: *Catalogue of Paintings and Engravings on View at the Rhode Island School of Design Opening of the New Galleries*, Museum of Art, Rhode Island School of Design, 1897; *Memorial Exhibition of Works of Art Given by Isaac Comstock Bates*, Museum of Art, Rhode Island School of Design, 1913, cat. no. 53.

52.
James David Smillie
American, 1833–1909

A Fallow Field, 1883
Etching. 12½″ x 19″

Gift of the Fazzano Brothers. 84.198.876.12

53.
James David Smillie (after Charles Emile Jacque)
American, 1833–1909

Landscape with Sheep, 1879
Etching. 12⅝″ x 9¾″

Gift of the Fazzano Brothers. 84.198.876.29

54.
Eugene L. Smyth
American, 1857–1932

A Shower, 1891
Signed at lower right: Eugene L. Smyth 1891
Oil on canvas. 10″ x 14″

Bequest of Isaac C. Bates. 13.950

Exhibitions: Providence Art Club, 1897; *Memorial Exhibition of
Works of Art Given by Isaac Comstock Bates*, Museum of Art, Rhode
Island School of Design, 1913, cat. no. 54.

55.
Dwight W. Tryon
American, 1849–1925

Daybreak, 1885
Signed at lower right: D. W. Tryon, 1885
Oil on panel. 17¾" x 30"

Jesse H. Metcalf Fund. 13.043

Provenance: Frederick Bonner; William T. Evans, New York, 1886; L. Crist Delmonico, 1900; M. Knoedler and Co., New York, 1912.

Publications: Henry C. White, *The Life and Art of Dwight William Tryon*, Boston and New York, 1930; Mandel/RISD, 1977, pp. 68–70.

Exhibitions: *Catalogue of the Thirty-Third Exhibition*, Boston Art Club, Boston, 1886, cat. no. 125; *World's Columbian Exposition*, Chicago, 1893; *International Exhibition*, Munich, 1895; American Art Galleries, New York, 1900, cat. no. 219; *Dwight W. Tryon: A Retrospective Exhibition*, Museum of Art, University of Connecticut, Storrs, 1971; *New Bedford and Old Dartmouth: A Portrait of a Region's Past*, Historical Society, New Bedford, Massachusetts, 1975, cat. no. 190.

56.
Elihu Vedder
American, 1836–1923

Italian Scene—Pompeo, 1877–79
Signed at upper left: Vedder 1879
Oil on canvas. 12½″ x 9¼″

Museum Works of Art. 55.151

Provenance: The artist, 1880; Alfred Lawrence Eames, Boston, 1951.

Publications: W. H. Bishop, "Elihu Vedder," *The American Art Review*, 1, 1880–81, p. 372; Regina Soria, *Elihu Vedder: American Visionary Artist in Rome*, Cranbury, New Jersey, 1970; Mandel/RISD, 1977, pp. 168–172.

Exhibitions: Samuel P. Avery (Gallery), New York, 1880; Williams and Everett, Boston, 1880; *Travelers in Arcadia, American Artists in Italy 1830–1875*, Detroit Institute of Arts, traveling exhibition, 1951; *Paintings and Drawings by Elihu Vedder*, Smithsonian Institution traveling exhibition, 1961; *Perceptions and Evocations: The Art of Elihu Vedder*, National Collection of Fine Arts, Smithsonian Institution, Washington, D.C., 1979, cat. no. 79.

57.
Carleton Wiggins
American, 1848–1932

Winter Evening in France, 1882
Signed at lower left: Carleton Wiggins. 1882
Oil on canvas. 23″ x 33″

Bequest of Austin King. 21.452

Publications: *Catalogue of the Autumn Exhibition*, Museum of Art, Rhode Island School of Design, 1904, cat. no. 41; Mandel/RISD, 1977, pp. 173–175.

Exhibitions: *Exhibition of Eminent American and Foreign Artists*, Providence Art Club, 1902; *Catalogue of the Autumn Exhibition*, Museum of Art, Rhode Island School of Design, 1904, cat. no. 41.

58.
Alexander H. Wyant
American, 1832–1892

Landscape, Morning, ca. 1882
Oil on canvas. 13″ x 17⅝″

Bequest of Isaac C. Bates. 13.807

Provenance: Bought from the artist by Isaac C. Bates in 1882–83.

Publications: Mandel/RISD, 1977, pp. 64–66; Robert S. Olpin, *Alexander Helwig Wyant, 1836–1892*, Salt Lake City, 1968, p. 21.

Exhibitions: *Third Annual Exhibition*, Providence Art Club, 1882, cat. no. 123; *Paintings and Engravings on View at the Rhode Island School of Design at the Opening of the New Galleries*, Museum of Art, Rhode Island School of Design, 1897, cat. no. 103; *Memorial Exhibition of Works of Art Given by Isaac Comstock Bates*, Museum of Art, Rhode Island School of Design, 1913, cat. no. 69.

59.
Alexander H. Wyant
American, 1836–1892

An October Day, ca. 1888
Signed at lower left: A H Wyant
Oil on canvas. 37″ x 49¼″

Gift of Mrs. Jesse H. Metcalf. 94.002

Provenance: Mrs. A. L. Wyant, New York, 1893; Ortgies and Co., Wyant Executor's Sale, New York, 1894, cat. no. 112; C. S. Gifford, 1894.

Publications: Eliot Clark, *Sixty Paintings by Alexander H. Wyant*, New York, 1920; Robert S. Olpin, *Alexander Helwig Wyant, 1836–1892*, Salt Lake City, 1968; Mandel/RISD, 1977, pp. 70–72.

Exhibitions: *16th Chicago Exposition*, Chicago, 1888; *World's Columbian Exposition*, Chicago, 1893; *Painting and Engravings on View at the Rhode Island School of Design at the Opening of the New Galleries*, Museum of Art, Rhode Island School of Design, 1897, cat. no. 104; *Alexander Helwig Wyant, 1836–1892*, Museum of Fine Arts, University of Utah, Salt Lake City, 1968, cat. no. 45.

60.
Alexander H. Wyant
American, 1832–1892

Landscape
Watercolor. 10ʺ x 12½ʺ

Bequest of Isaac C. Bates. 13.814

Exhibition: *A History of American Water Color Painting*, Whitney
Museum of American Art, New York, 1942.